PLANET FOOTBALL

GREATEST MANAGERS

CONT

First published in paperback
in 2017 by Wayland
Copyright © Wayland, 2017
All rights reserved

Editor: Victoria Brooker
Produced for Wayland by
Tall Tree Ltd
Designer: Gary Hyde
Editor: Jon Richards

Dewey number: 796.3'34'0922-
dc23
ISBN 978 1 5263 0360 8

Wayland, an imprint of
Hachette Children's Group
Part of Hodder and Stoughton
Carmelite House
50 Victoria Embankment
London EC4Y 0DZ
An Hachette UK Company
www.hachette.co.uk
www.hachettechildrens.co.uk

FSC
Printed and bound in China
10 9 8 7 6 5 4 3 2 1

FOOTBALL COACHES

Football teams need someone to organise them, pick the 11 players that start the game and decide how they should line-up and play against their opponents. This is the job of the club's head coach or manager. It is a high-pressure role.

LAURENTIU REGHECAMPF

At some clubs, especially in the UK and in the past, a football manager had control over both the team and other aspects of a football club, such as the buying and selling of players. Today, many top clubs have a head coach instead who focuses on training, tactics and preparing the players for matches. Many of these head coaches only have a limited say about player transfers.

Laurentiu Reghecampf, head coach of Steaua Bucharest, is thrown into the air by his delighted players after winning the Romanian league in 2014. It was Reghecampf and Steaua's second league title in a row. In the two seasons, and 68 league games, his side only lost four matches.

4

LUIS ENRIQUE

Players may get the bigger share of the glory when their team wins a competition, but coaches also get applause and praise. Fierce ambition burns inside every top football coach. It is their dream to mould a team of players into a side that wins major trophies. The very best coaches are extremely well paid and highly sought after, as it's believed they can make the difference to a team's chances of success.

After managing the Barcelona B team and stints in Italy with Roma and Spain with Celta, Luis Enrique returned to Barcelona where he won the treble (league, cup and Champions league) during his first year in charge.

"A COACH OR MANAGER IS A GUIDE. HE TAKES A GROUP OF PEOPLE AND SAYS, 'WITH YOU I CAN MAKE US A SUCCESS; I CAN SHOW YOU THE WAY.'"
ARSÈNE WENGER

JUST THE JOB

A coach does far more than just pick the team for a match. He or she must work with the squad in daily training; deal with tired, unfit or unhappy players; pick the right tactics for the game; sometimes deal with fans and officials, as well as hold press conferences to inform the media.

Top coaches watch hours of footage of their opponents, looking for any weaknesses. Discussions with assistant coaches may aid the head coach as he picks both the players and tactics with which he will start the game. Coaches can also alter tactics during a game, such as moving a midfield player into attack or stiffening the defence by playing a defensive midfielder in front of them.

DIDIER DESCHAMPS

France coach, Didier Deschamps (right) stands with the rest of his coaching team. A modern head coach is in charge of a team of staff. These may include medics, a dietician and physiotherapists as well as assistant coaches who may specialise in certain skills such as goalkeeping.

PEP GUARDIOLA

Bayern Munich coach Pep Guardiola gives Franck Ribery last-minute instructions as he heads onto the pitch. A coach can replace up to three players in most competitions with players off the bench.

A coach can use substitutes to replace an injured player or change the way his team is playing. Sometimes, attackers prove super-subs as they score goals to win the game, but other substitutes can be just as crucial. At the 2014 World Cup, Louis Van Gaal brought on Tim Krul as a substitute goalkeeper just for the penalty shootout. He was proven right when Krul saved two penalties as the Netherlands beat Costa Rica.

FABIO CAPELLO

"WE ALL THOUGHT TIM WAS THE BEST KEEPER TO STOP PENALTIES. HE IS TALLER AND HAS A LONGER REACH. IT WORKED OUT. THAT WAS BEAUTIFUL."
LOUIS VAN GAAL

IN THE MARKET

Thousands of players change clubs and these transfers can make or break a coach's reign. Although coaches at big clubs may recommend who to buy, the final decision may rest with others such as the technical director.

Some coaches are well-known for picking up bargains. Sir Alex Ferguson spent just £550,000 on top goalkeeper, Peter Schmeichel, while Arsène Wenger's Arsenal paid only £500,000 for Nicolas Anelka and sold him two years later to Real Madrid for £23 million.

DIEGO SIMEONE

Diego Simeone played 106 times for Argentina and took his competitive attitude into the transfer market. At Atlético Madrid, he has repeatedly bought cheap and sold dearly, yet won the UEFA Europa League and the Spanish league title.

In recent times, Atlético Madrid coach, Diego Simeone has an excellent transfer record. His club sold Radamel Falcao, David De Gea, Sergio Aguero and Diego Costa for nearly £140 million, yet found good replacements for a fraction of that cost.

FOOTBALL ICONS

NAME: .... BRIAN CLOUGH
DATE OF BIRTH: 21/03/1935
NATIONALITY: .... BRITISH

Outspoken and strong-willed, Brian Clough coached Derby to their first ever league championship in 1973. At Nottingham Forest, he created a team that won promotion to the first division in 1977, won the league the following year and in 1979 and 1980 won back-to-back European Cups.

SERGIO AGUERO

NEYMAR

An astute coach can sometimes borrow promising players from other clubs for all or part of a season. These loan signings can make an impact such as Romelu Lukaku scoring 17 goals for West Bromwich Albion in the 2012–13 season while on loan from Chelsea.

Brazilian forward Neymar moved from Santos to Barcelona in 2013. Although details of his transfer have been kept secret, it is rumoured that the Spanish club paid up to £45 million for him.

"WE TALK ABOUT IT FOR 20 MINUTES AND THEN WE DECIDE I WAS RIGHT."
BRIAN CLOUGH ON LISTENING TO HIS PLAYERS' OPINIONS ON HOW TO PLAY

LEAGUE LEGENDS

Every country in the world runs its own football league, with the top club becoming league champions. Top club coaches strive to win league titles and some have been extremely successful.

After winning the Scottish league three times with Aberdeen, Alex Ferguson enjoyed spectacular success at Manchester United. Famed for his competitiveness, for his attacking football and for developing many young players, including David Beckham, Ryan Giggs and Cristiano Ronaldo, Ferguson won 13 Premier League championships before retiring in 2013.

SIR ALEX FERGUSON

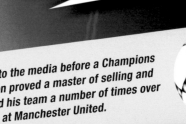

Sir Alex Ferguson talks to the media before a Champions League match. Ferguson proved a master of selling and buying players to rebuild his team a number of times over his 27 years at Manchester United.

Coaches know that a season in the league is a long one. In most of the top leagues of Europe, there are 34, 36 or 38 games. Successful league coaches overcome dips in their team's form and poor results, sometimes getting wins even when their team is not playing at its best.

OTTMAR HITZFELD

Ottmar Hitzfeld is the Bundesliga's most successful coach. He guided Borussia Dortmund to two championships and then took Bayern to five more between 1998–99 and 2007–08. He has also won two Swiss Super League titles with Grasshopper Club Zürich.

"I'VE NEVER PLAYED FOR A DRAW IN MY LIFE."
SIR ALEX FERGUSON

NUMBERS GAME

1,500

The number of matches Sir Alex Ferguson managed Manchester United for. His side won 895 and drew 338 of these matches.

GIOVANNI TRAPATTONI

Giovanni Trapattoni has coached nine different clubs in Portugal, Germany, Austria and Italy. In each country, he has won the league at least once. The Italian has won Serie A with both Inter or Juventus a record seven times – more than any other coach.

CHAMPIONS LEAGUE COACHES

A competition for the best football clubs in Europe began in 1955 as the European Cup. In 1992, it received a makeover as the UEFA Champions League and is now the biggest prize in club football.

⚽ Qualifying for the Champions League can be worth tens of millions of pounds for a club, especially if they progress to the later rounds of the competition. Coaches at top clubs in Europe are under pressure as they are often judged by how well their teams do in the Champions League.

NUMBERS GAME

5

The number of coaches who have won the Champions League with two different clubs.

JUPP HEYNCKES

The veteran coach first won the Champions League in 1998 at Real Madrid, the sixth club he had been in charge of. In his third spell as head coach of Bayern Munich, Heynckes guided them to a sensational 2012–13 season, winning the German Cup, the Bundesliga and the Champions League.

FOOTBALL ICONS

NAME: BOB PAISLEY
DATE OF BIRTH: 23/01/1919
NATIONALITY: BRITISH

After retiring as a player, Paisley became Liverpool's physiotherapist and later a coach under manager, Bill Shankly, before taking charge in 1974. In the next nine seasons under his command, Liverpool won an amazing 20 major trophies including the European Cup three times in 1977, 1978 and 1981.

A team in the Champions League has to play midweek games in the competition as well as the league and cup games in their own country at weekends. This glut of games gives coaches a real headache. They must manage their squad and sometimes take the risk of dropping star players to rest them shortly before a crucial Champions League match.

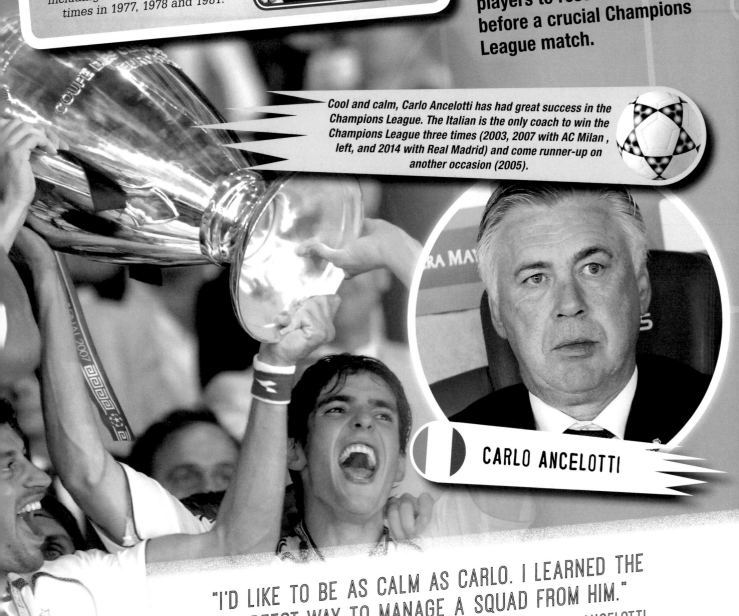

Cool and calm, Carlo Ancelotti has had great success in the Champions League. The Italian is the only coach to win the Champions League three times (2003, 2007 with AC Milan, left, and 2014 with Real Madrid) and come runner-up on another occasion (2005).

CARLO ANCELOTTI

"I'D LIKE TO BE AS CALM AS CARLO. I LEARNED THE PERFECT WAY TO MANAGE A SQUAD FROM HIM."
ITALIAN FOOTBALLER, ALESSANDRO COSTACURTA ON CARLO ANCELOTTI

UP-AND-COMING COMING COACHES

Going into coaching is the next step for many professional footballers when they retire from playing. Only a handful, though, gain the skills, opportunities and success to build a strong second career in football as a promising head coach.

SLAVEN BILIC

Many ex-players learn on the job by working as assistants to a club's head coach. They build experience and may eventually leave to become a head coach elsewhere or, occasionally, are promoted and made head coach when their former boss leaves.

After coaching his hometown club, Hadjuk Split, Slaven Bilic was appointed head coach of Croatia in 2006. During his six years in charge, Croatia only lost 8 of their 65 games, making him a hot property when he entered club management. In 2015, he took charge of West Ham United.

Many ambitious coaches eye jobs at bigger clubs or in bigger leagues. The top five leagues of Europe, in England, France, Germany, Italy and Spain, are where many of the world's top footballers play and up-and-coming coaches are keen to work with them. But they face strong competition from others to convince top clubs to appoint them.

VITOR PEREIRA

Vitor Pereira was an assistant to Porto head coach, André Villas-Boas until Villas-Boas left to take charge of Chelsea. Porto made Pereira their new head coach and he responded by delivering two Portuguese league championships in a row.

FRANK DE BOER

NUMBERS GAME

9

The number of Eredivisie titles Frank de Boer has won as both a player or a coach.

Frank de Boer was made caretaker manager of Ajax in 2010. Leading the club to win the Eredivisie (Dutch league) that season, he was made permanent. Ajax then won the league for the next three seasons, confirming de Boer as a rising star.

"HE'S EXCELLENT AT TAKING A GROUP OF YOUNG, TALENTED INDIVIDUALS AND TURNING THEM INTO A WELL-FUNCTIONING TEAM."
DUTCH FOOTBALL EXPERT ELKO BORN ON FRANK DE BOER

CLUB AND COUNTRY

Success at club level can see a coach considered for the role of head coach of a national team. If appointed, a coach can expect a different way of working from running a club team.

National teams play far fewer games than club sides, as little as ten matches in any year that does not feature a major tournament. While a national coach can potentially pick any player from that country, they have limited time to work directly with the players before each match. They tend to watch plenty of matches to look at players they might want to pick.

DIDIER DESCHAMPS

A World Cup winner in 1998 with France, Didier Deschamps coached Monaco, Juventus and Marseilles before becoming head coach of France in 2012. By June 2015, he had led his team to 21 wins and just eight losses in 37 games.

Fabio Capello coached the England national team from 2008 to 2012 and then became head coach of Russia. Bora Milutinovic has coached national teams as varied as Jamaica and Iraq in a long career.

NUMBERS GAME

66.67

The win percentage that Fabio Capello achieved as England coach (28 wins in 42 games).

FABIO CAPELLO

BORA MILUTINOVIC

Some national team coaches are appointed for short periods with the aim of qualifying for a major competition such as the World Cup or European Championships. Serbian coach, Bora Milutinovic coached China to reach their first ever World Cup in 2002. It was the fifth national team he had coached to qualify for a World Cup (Mexico, Nigeria, Costa Rica and USA).

MORTEN OLSEN

While most national coaches stay for 2–4 years, Morten Olsen has been head coach of Denmark since 2000. He is the only person to have reached the milestone of 100 matches as a player and as a coach of the same national team.

WORLD CUP COACHES

The FIFA World Cup, held once every four years, is the world's biggest single-sport event. Watched by hundreds of millions of TV viewers, the month-long tournament determines the best national football team on the planet.

Some 200 countries want to take part in each FIFA World Cup but only 32 make it. So, the first hurdle the coaches and their teams have to overcome is a series of qualifying games against rivals. If they qualify, a coach has a number of months and a series of friendly matches to decide which 23 players will make up his World Cup squad.

After coaching Real Madrid to two Champions League successes, Vincente del Bosque became head coach of Spain in 2008. He won his first 10 games in charge and masterminded his team's triumphs at the 2010 World Cup and the European Championships two years later.

VINCENTE DEL BOSQUE

Once at the tournament, coaches know that the time for experimenting is over. They need to win games to stay in the competition. A defeat in the first game, though, doesn't have to mean failure. In their first match of the 2010 World Cup, Spain under Vincente del Bosque lost to Switzerland but went on to win the tournament.

A successful club coaching career in Italy saw Marcello Lippi appointed Italy's head coach for the 2006 World Cup. Lippi blended a team of experienced players together well to reach the final where they beat France to win the World Cup.

MARCELLO LIPPI

NUMBERS GAME

0

The number of the qualifying games for the 2010 and 2014 World Cup that Germany lost with Joachim Löw in charge – 17 wins and three draws.

The victorious German team celebrate winning the 2014 World Cup. Their coach, Joachim Löw, masterminded their campaign which included an epic 7-1 thrashing of the hosts Brazil in the semi-final and a narrow win over Argentina in the final.

JOACHIM LÖW

"WE STARTED THIS PROJECT TEN YEARS AGO AND WHAT HAS HAPPENED TODAY IS THE RESULT OF MANY YEARS' WORK."
JOACHIM LÖW ON WINNING THE 2014 WORLD CUP

DOING IT THEIR WAY

Some coaches build a reputation for doing things differently. It might be how they behave in front of the world's media or unusual attitudes to training. These coaches have had success doing things their own way.

Becoming head coach of Porto in 2002, Mourinho has been a success ever since, winning the Champions League with Porto and moving to Chelsea where he won two Premier League titles. After successful spells at Inter Milan and Real Madrid, he returned to Chelsea guiding them to the Premier League title again in 2014–15.

JOSÉ MOURINHO

Mourinho is unpredictable and often entertaining in media interviews. In April 2015, he stated that he would sell star midfielder, Eden Hazard, but at a price of £100 million per leg!

Jürgen Klopp is an emotional and passionate coach who forms a powerful bond with club supporters and believes in attacking football. He can surprise players and fans with unusual methods such as taking the players training in a public park. In 2015, Klopp left Borussia Dortmund to take a break from football.

While at Dortmund, Jürgen Klopp regularly challenged Bayern Munich's dominance, winning the Bundesliga twice (2010–11, 2011–12) and reaching the final of the 2012–13 Champions League.

NUMBERS GAME

22

The number of major trophies including two Champions League titles that José Mourinho won between 2003 and 2015.

JÜRGEN KLOPP

"THERE IS NO PRESSURE AT THE TOP. THE PRESSURE'S BEING SECOND OR THIRD"
JOSÉ MOURINHO

DUTCH MASTERS

The Netherlands is a relatively small country with a population around a quarter of the UK. Yet, it has produced a large number of superb players and excellent coaches.

RONALD KOEMAN

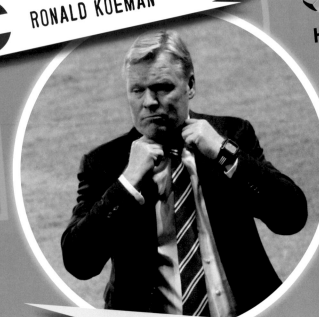

Many top Dutch coaches from Ronald Koeman to Guus Hiddink began their coaching career in the Dutch leagues. The top division in the Netherlands is called the Eredivisie and a Dutch coach who wins this competition is often offered a job with a club in one of the top European leagues in Germany, Spain, Italy or England.

Ronald Koeman served as assistant coach of the Dutch national team and at Barcelona before striking out on his own. He has won three Eredivisie titles, two with Ajax and one with PSV Eindhoven, before joining Southampton in 2014.

22

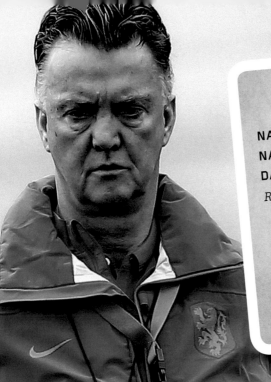

FOOTBALL ICONS

NAME: .... RINUS MICHELS

NATIONALITY: .... DUTCH

DATE OF BIRTH: ... 09/02/1928

Rinus Michels coached Ajax to win their first ever European Cup in 1971 after four Eredivisie titles in the 1960s. He took the Dutch national team to their first ever World Cup final in 1974 and, in his third spell in charge of the Dutch team, in 1988 won the European Championship. He was named FIFA Coach of the Century in 1999.

LOUIS VAN GAAL

Coaches from the Netherlands have been in great demand ever since Rinus Michels introduced 'total football' in the 1960s as coach of Ajax and later, the Dutch national team and Barcelona. This flowing, attacking style of play sees players swap positions frequently throughout a game. Since that time, Dutch teams have had a reputation for flair and skill.

Louis Van Gaal has won the Eredivisie four times with two different clubs, Ajax and AZ Alkmaar. He also had success in Spain with Barcelona and in Germany with Bayern Munich. He also coached the Netherlands national team to third place at the 2014 FIFA World Cup.

"I LIKE LOUIS AND HAVE ALWAYS HAD A GOOD RAPPORT WITH HIM. IF I HAD TO CHOOSE ONE WORD FOR HIM IT WOULD BE 'FORMIDABLE'."

SIR ALEX FERGUSON ON LOUIS VAN GAAL

FEMALE COACHES

NUMBERS GAME

89.7

The win percentage of the US women's team when Pia Mariane Sundhage was in charge.

Women's football is booming, and more than five times as many women play football today than in 1985. But only some of its clubs or national sides have been run by female coaches. Here are three of the most pioneering and successful.

CORINNE DIACRE

Many national female football teams have been managed by men, but some have had a women as a head coach. One of the most successful is Silvia Neid who became the first female coach to win the Women's World Cup with Germany in 2007. She has also led Germany to win two European Championships in 2009 and 2013.

SILVIA NEID

German coach Silvia Neid attends a press conference during a tournament in Portugal in 2015. In 2010, Neid became the first to win FIFA's World Coach in Women's Football award.

PIA MARIANE SUNDHAGE

After retiring from playing, Pia Mariane Sundhage coached women's teams in Norway, Sweden and the USA before leading the US women's team to two Olympic gold medals. She was appointed coach of Sweden for the 2015 Women's World Cup.

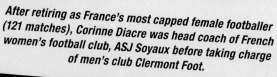
After retiring as France's most capped female footballer (121 matches), Corinne Diacre was head coach of French women's football club, ASJ Soyaux before taking charge of men's club Clermont Foot.

Opportunities for female coaches in male football have been extremely rare but are slowly starting to occur. The former coach of Arsenal Ladies team, Shelley Kerr, was made head coach of Lowland League men's team, Stirling University FC in 2014. In the same year, Corinne Diacre was appointed head coach of Clermont Foot, a professional men's football club who play in France's Ligue 2.

"I'M TRYING TO MAINTAIN MY FOCUS — WHAT INTERESTS ME IS THAT MY PLAYERS TAKE THE LIMELIGHT, NOT ME."
CORINNE DIACRE BEFORE HER FIRST GAME AS HEAD COACH OF CLERMONT FOOT

COACHING WITH STYLE

Some coaches focus on gaining results at all costs. Others, like Arsène Wenger and Pep Guardiola believe in playing a particular brand of attacking football which calls for plenty of skill and vision.

Josép 'Pep' Guardiola's first club as a player and coach was Barcelona. He took charge of the Spanish giants in 2008 and made an immediate impact, winning La Liga, the Champions League and the Spanish Cup in his first season. In 2012, and after winning 14 trophies in just four years in charge, the hottest property in football coaching left Barcelona to take time off before taking charge of German giants, Bayern Munich the following year.

PEP GUARDIOLA

At the age of 38, Guardiola became the youngest coach to win the UEFA Champions League in 2009. He guided Barcelona to a second Champions League triumph two years later.

Arsène Wenger coached in Japan and took Monaco to the French league title before joining Arsenal in 1996. He changed the diet and training of players at the London club and has made a series of shrewd buys. Under his coaching, some players have had their careers transformed such as Thierry Henry, who went from under-performing winger to deadly striker and Arsenal's all-time leading goalscorer.

NUMBERS GAME
319
The number of wins or draws out of the 355 games that Guardiola has been in charge of Barcelona and Bayern Munich (2008–May 2015).

With the retirement of Sir Alex Ferguson, Arsène Wenger is the longest-serving coach in the Premier League. He has coached Arsenal for more than 1,050 games, won the Premier League three times and the FA Cup six times.

ARSÈNE WENGER

"WHAT MOTIVATES ME IS AN IDEAL OF THINKING ABOUT HOW FOOTBALL SHOULD BE. AND TO TRY TO GET NEAR THIS WAY OF PLAYING."
ARSÈNE WENGER

GLOBETROTTING COACHES

In the past, only a small number of coaches travelled abroad to coach foreign national teams or clubs. Today, coaches rack up the air miles as they switch continents to work all over the world.

PHIL SCOLARI

Europe and South America have long been the powerhouses of world football. Teams from these two continents, for example, have won every World Cup since the first in 1930. So, European and South American coaches have often been sought after by teams in emerging football nations in Africa and Asia.

The much-travelled Brazilian coach Luiz Felipe Scolari has coached 21 clubs in places as far afield as Saudi Arabia, Uzbekistan and Japan. 'Big Phil' has been head coach of Brazil in two separate spells. His first in 2001–02 saw Brazil win the 2002 World Cup.

JÜRGEN KLINSMANN

German striker, Jürgen Klinsmann, moved to the USA after he retired. He became head coach of the German national team, taking them to third place in the 2006 World Cup. In 2011, he was made head coach of the US national team winning the CONCACAF Gold Cup in 2013.

GUUS HIDDINK

Dutch coach Guus Hiddink has been in demand ever since he won five Dutch league titles with PSV Eindhoven. He has coached national teams on three continents including the Netherlands, Australia, Turkey, Russia and South Korea whom he took to fourth place at the 2002 World Cup.

Coaches working abroad may have to deal with a different language and culture in their new workplace but many foreign coaches have had great success. French coach, Hervé Renard, for example, guided Zambia to win the 2012 African Cup of Nations. In 2015, he repeated the feat, this time as head coach of the Ivory Coast.

"I CONSIDER KOREA MY SECOND HOME COUNTRY AFTER THE EXPERIENCES OF 2002. I ALWAYS FEEL RATHER SPECIAL WHEN I COME BACK."
GUUS HIDDINK

QUIZ

1. Which coach led Germany to win the 2014 FIFA World Cup?

2. Sergio Aguero, David De Gea and Diego Costa all played for which Spanish club?

3. Which female coach won the 2007 Women's World Cup and the 2009 and 2013 European Championships?

4. Can you name either of the national teams that Hervé Renard coached to win the African Cup of Nations?

5. With which club did Sir Alex Ferguson win the Scottish league championship?

6. Who is the youngest coach to win the UEFA Champions League?

7. Who was coach of Bayern Munich in the 2012-13 season when they won the German league, German Cup and UEFA Champions League?

8. How many clubs has Luiz Felipe Scolari coached up until May 2015?

WEBSITES AND BOOKS

http://www.fifa.com/classicfootball/coaches/
Detailed biographies of some of the most important and successful football coaches.

http://news.bbc.co.uk/sport1/hi/academy/4354156.stm
A short article on the skills needed to be a good coach.

http://www.espnfc.co.uk/blog/espn-fc-united-blog/68/post/2077039/espn-fc-ranks-europes-top-20-football-managers
Short but interesting profiles of 20 of the best football coaches from around the world.

http://www.bbc.co.uk/sport/0/football/28939359
See how transfer fees have risen with this table and article on record footballer transfers in the UK.

Truth or Busted: Football
by Adam Sutherland (Wayland, 2014)

Radar Top Jobs: Being a Professional Footballer by Sarah Levete (Wayland, 2013)

Football Joke Book
by Clive Gifford (Wayland, 2013)

GLOSSARY

Bundesliga
The German league competition.

CONCACAF Gold Cup
A tournament for national teams from North and Central America and the Caribbean.

FIFA
Short for the Fédération Internationale de Football Association, the organisation that runs world football.

friendly
A football match not played as any part of a competition.

La Liga
The top league for clubs in Spain.

physiotherapist
A person who uses massage and other physical treatments to keep footballers fit and to help injured players recover.

professional
To be paid to play sport.

red card
A card shown to a player by a referee to signal that the player has been sent off the pitch.

scout
A person who watches games either featuring opposing teams or players a club might want to sign and reports back to a head coach.

Serie A
The top division of the Italian football league.

squad
All the players that a coach can select from to make a team of 11 players that start a match plus substitutes.

substitution
When one player leaves the game and is replaced by a fresh player due to injury or a change of team tactics.

transfer
When a footballer moves from one club to another, often with a fee paid by the buying team.

UEFA Champions League
A competition for Europe's leading clubs held every year.

ANSWERS

1. Joachim Löw
2. Atlético Madrid
3. Silvia Neid
4. Zambia, Ivory Coast
5. Aberdeen
6. Pep Guardiola
7. Jupp Heynckes
8. 21

31

INDEX

The publisher would like to thank the following for their kind permission to reproduce their photographs:
Key: (t) top; (c) centre; (b) bottom; (l) left; (r) right
All images **Dreamstime.com** unless otherwise indicated.
6-7 (c) A.RICARDO/Shutterstock.com; 9 (t) Nationaal Archief, Den Haag/Creative Commons share Alike; 11 (t) Biso/Creative Commons;
13 (t) Eric The Fish/Creative Commons; 17(t) Antonio Scorza/Shutterstock.com; 20-21(c) mooinblack/Shutterstock.com;
22-23 (c) AGIF/Shutterstock.com; 24-25(c) GettyImages/Jean Catuffe; 28 (l) Danilo Borges/copa2014.gov.br Licença
Creative Commons Atribuição 3.0 Brasil; 29(t) Steindy/GNU Free Documentation